LIFE AND LE___

EDITED BY DESMOND MacCARTHY

VOL. VII. No. 41. OCTOBER 1931

CONTENTS

	Page
SAMUEL BUTLER By the Editor	235
CHARLES PAINE PAULI AND SAMUEL BUTLER	252
UNPUBLISHED EXTRACTS FROM THE NOTE-BOOKS OF SAMUEL BUTLER With the permission of Mr. A. T. Bartholomew	300

LIFE AND LETTERS

THE EDITOR

SAMUEL BUTLER

When *Life and Letters* started, we said that from time to time we would devote a number either to a single contribution, or to a single subject. Accordingly, in August 1929 we published Mr. Richard Hughes' brilliant novel, *A High Wind in Jamaica;* and now we offer not this time a work of art, but a number concerned with one writer. This is a 'Samuel Butler' number. It contains his own account of his friendship with Charles Pauli, a curious story, never completely published before, and some unpublished extracts from his 'Note Books'.

I

Samuel Butler played a not unimportant part in my own education (I made his acquaintance when I was ten years old), and later my work as a journalist and critic was often concerned with his books. In 1909 I edited a periodical called *The New Quarterly*, and Festing Jones gave me for it extracts from Samuel Butler's 'Note Books'. Butler was not yet famous. When he died, in June 1902, the measure of his reputation was given by an article in *The Times*, regretting that so talented a man had not done more. That estimate seemed later beside and far below the mark. Samuel Butler was one of those rare, incontestable personalities in literature, who affect permanently the thought and temper of all predisposed to their influence; indeed, the first impression made on anyone reading his 'Note Books', which date from the 'sixties, may well be that many of Butler's ideas are those which are at the present moment 'in the air', and by 'in the air', of course, people mean in the papers or other men's books.

Later, Bernard Shaw pointed out his own debt to him in his Preface to *Major Barbara*, which was one of the earliest and most effective statements of Butler's claim to wider recognition. In this Preface, Mr. Shaw insisted that Butler 'In his own department was one of the greatest writers of the nineteenth century'.

As a moralist, Butler was a confirmed hedonist and Laodicean; *surtout point de zèle*, he believed was the finest motto ever coined for humanity. He really and utterly believed that compromise was the guide to life; he saw compromise written over the face of all creation. And not only in action, but in thought, right behaviour and truth were best obtained by combining the conflicting reports of faith and reason. The blend was only perfectly satisfactory when the balance was reached unconsciously; every philosophy was nonsense when ridden home, and every moral ideal which outsoared the practice of averagely good men was suspect. Scattered up and down his books are aphorisms to the effect that a man whose mind is of the right temper must be uncertain in spite of uncertainty, and uncertain in spite of certainty, which in practice comes to something like having a sense of humour, for it is characteristic of humour to hold together, at the same moment, the profound and superficial,

the doubtful and the obvious, the serious and the indifferent aspects of things. The favourite virtue of the
humorist is always toleration: it was Butler's favourite
virtue, too.

The most comprehensive description of Samuel Butler
as a writer is, then, that he was a humorous philosopher.
The interdependence of his philosophy and his humour
is, indeed, often so complete that it is puzzling to decide
whether he was a philosopher who chanced upon explana-
tions which would justify humour, or a born humorist
who set out in search of a philosophy to explain the way
things naturally struck him. Both processes had a share
in his work. He saw jokes where no one else saw them,
because, sceptical and curious, he looked at everything
in his own way; and things would occur to him first as
jokes which afterwards impressed him as perfectly true.
Butler's sense of humour often performed the service for
him that the dove did for Noah in the ark. It flew out into
the unknown, bringing back to him an indication that he
would soon find solid ground beneath his feet. The
humorous philosopher is rare, but when he does appear
his influence quickly spreads. We laugh with him, not
taking him seriously, and lo! we have already caught his
way of thinking.

I made Butler's acquaintance at a hotel in the valley
of the Saas in Switzerland, where I was staying with my
parents. Opposite us at *table d'hote* sat an elderly man with
very bushy black eyebrows, and with him, from time to
time, they interchanged a few cheerful polite remarks.
A day or two later I happened to feel an extreme reluc-
tance to notice the bell which announced the midday
meal, and instead of going in I continued to clamber about
the valley rocks. After a short interval I saw what I knew

I should see next, my mother appearing at the door of the hotel frantically waving her parasol. This was a signal which could not be ignored like the bell. She had evidently waited until lunch had well begun, and then, losing patience, come out to fetch me. I was not surprised. What did surprise me was that she was presently followed by the old gentleman with the thick eyebrows. As we all three entered the hotel together he whispered: 'I thought I'd better come, with a stranger Mama could not be quite so angry'. It was only long afterwards that I realized that it was kind of an elderly gentleman to jump up from his midday meal and hurry out into the blazing sun to prevent a small boy from getting a scolding; but when I did, I realized also that it was thoroughly characteristic of him to suppose that *every* child was likely to be bullied by its parents. (Readers of *The Way of All Flesh* will understand.) After that, I used often to go sketching with him. No doubt while he sketched and I lay beside his easel he talked wisely, but I heeded him not. I cannot remember a scrap of our conversations. But I do remember that on Sunday mornings at breakfast he used to say: 'Do you think Mr. Selwyn would mind (Mr. Selwyn was the chaplain, and in those days every hotel haunted by the British had its chaplain), do you think Mr. Selwyn would forgive us if we did *not* go to church?' (He had been pleased to find that my favourite text was 'And now to God the Father, God the Son, etc.') And off we would go together. If our acquaintance had ended there I should have little to tell, but later, when I was in London, I used sometimes to go and see him in his rooms at Clifford's Inn. I was dimly aware that he was a remarkable man— but that was not the sort of fact which interested me. I only divined it from the interest my father took in his conversation, while I ate nuts and apples and listened. Mr. Butler would sometimes give me one of his books, always with strict injunctions not to attempt to read it.

As I grew older I began to go and see him by myself. He often talked in a way which both puzzled me and amused me, giving me advice of which I could make nothing at the time, advice which did not agree at all with that of my masters and pastors. For instance, he would say, looking at me gravely: 'As long as you tell no lies to yourself and are kind, you may lie and lie and lie and yet not be untrue to any man'. Once I remember giving up the last two hours of the Eton and Harrow match—it's true the result was a foregone conclusion—in order to go and see him. Instead of sitting and keeping the bowling averages, I went off to listen to his talk, which, I take it, is one of the greatest compliments ever paid to a philosopher in England. I must have been seventeen then, I was beginning to understand him.

In stature he was a small man, but you hardly noticed that. His slightly built frame was disguised in clothes of enviable bagginess and of a clumsy conventional cut, and he wore prodigiously roomy boots. But it was the hirsute, masculine vigour of his head which prevented you from thinking him a small man. Indeed, it was a surprise to me to hear afterwards that he had coxed at Cambridge the St. John's boat: I had remembered him, it seemed, as even rather a heavy man. His company manner was that of a kind old gentleman, prepared to be a little shocked by any disregard of the proprieties; the sort of old gentleman who is very mild in reproof, but whose quiet insistence that everybody should behave properly is most soothing to elderly ladies of limited means. He spoke softly and slowly, often with his head a little down, looking gravely over his spectacles and pouting his lips, and with a deliberate demureness so disarming that he was able to utter the most subversive sentiments without exciting more than a moment's astonishment. The next, his companion was completely reassured. 'No, Mr. Butler could not have meant that. I wasn't quite quick enough. Mr. Butler is such an *original* man.' Such was the impression he made on circumspect, humdrum people. It was comic to anyone who knew what a bull in a china shop he really was. And though he was a great adept at poking gentle fun at people, he never snubbed them or scored off them. In fact, he had a strong abhorrence to anything of that kind. I think he enjoyed, a little, the irony which resides in perfect politeness, but politeness was not in the least a pose on his part. It sprang from his dislike of overbearingness. To take advantage of superiority of intellect, or any other kind of superiority, moral force, knowledge of the world, reputation, wealth, social position, a fine manner, and to use it to browbeat a helpless person was in his eyes a revolting, unpardonable offence. I heard him often use the word 'caddish', and it always stigmatized that kind of behaviour. If I were to mention the names of those he called 'cads' the list would cause great surprise. Besides, he liked mediocre, humdrum people; they were at any rate freer from this odious sin than the intellectual and successful.

I asked him once if he were any relation to the late Master of Trinity, Dr. Butler. 'What!' he exclaimed with soft and gentle emphasis, '*that* beastly cad!' It took me a moment or two to rearrange my ideas—on the Master, caddishness, Samuel Butler himself! Then I guessed: Dr. Butler's eighteenth-century suavity might easily strike his namesake as coming suspiciously near an attempt to play

him off the social stage, though in the Master's case it was
nothing of the kind. Perhaps—I knew they had met after
Samuel Butler's *Authoress of the Odyssey* had appeared—
the Master had asked him, accidentally and sweetly,
some question about Nausicaa equivalent in its effect
to his famous invitation at a Trinity Lodge musical
party, 'So pleased you have come. Won't you take a
back seat?'

The last time I saw him was at a dinner at the Albe-
marle Club, given more or less in his honour. It was in
the winter before he died, and he was already very tired.
He made, I remember, a little fun of an intense lady there
who declared that Art was more to her than Nature. He
was not always very quick to see the point when others
poked fun at him. I remember his coming back from a
visit to Lady Ritchie, who was as good a hand as he at
gentle irony, telling me with amazement that she had
said: 'Mr. Butler, I will tell you my theory about the
sonnets (Butler had just published his *Authoress of the
Odyssey*, and was about to publish his book on the
Sonnets): I believe they were written to Shakespeare by
Ann Hathaway.' 'Poor lady,' Butler went on, 'that *was*
a stupid thing to say!'

II

The importance of money as the means to a good life is a
theme which Butler constantly and vehemently empha-
sized. The emphasis he laid on it is one of the character-
istics which made him an original moralist and so acute a
commentator on life. Everybody, according to Butler,
must have money on the brain so long as that brain is in
reasonable condition. 'Though Wisdom cannot be gotten
for gold, still less can it be gotten without it. Gold, or the

value which is equivalent to gold, lies at the root of Wisdom.' ('Note Books', p. 172.) For the modern Simony, which 'is not dealing in livings but the thinking they can buy the Holy Ghost for money, which vulgar rich people indulge in when they dabble in literature, music and painting', he felt deep contempt. But anyone who refused to admit that a *discreta posizionina* was an unmixed blessing he despised quite as much, and thought much more dangerous. He was fond of following up this idea: his handling of it is an example of his method.

The rich man to him was the hundred-handed Gyges of the poets. He alone possessed the full complement of limbs who stood at the summit of opulence. Reckoned by his horse-power, a Rockefeller is the most astonishing organism the world has ever seen; and therefore, according to Butler, the deep impression wealth makes on the imagination is reasonable, and the respect with which we so often treat those who are richer than ourselves a legitimate feeling. 'It is,' he characteristically added, 'the same sort of affectionate reverence which a dog feels for a man, and is not infrequently manifested in a similar manner.' Thus, to abuse the rich, provided they are amiable, handsome, and considerate, revolted his common sense.

People ask complainingly what swells have done, or do for society, that they should be able to live without working. The good swell is the creature towards which all nature has been groaning and travailing together until now. He is an ideal. He shows what may be done in the way of good breeding, health, looks, temper, and fortune. He realises men's dreams of themselves, at any rate vicariously. He preaches the gospel of grace. The world is like a spoilt child: it has this good thing given to it at great expense and then says it is useless!' ('Note Books', pp. 35–6.)

It was, however, not the 'swell' whom he himself considered the finest type. 'I suppose,' he wrote, 'an Italian peasant or a Breton, Norman or English fisherman, is about the best thing Nature does in the way of men—the richer and the poorer being alike mistakes.' Still, he would have no blaspheming against Mammon. This is one of the points at which the thought of Samuel Butler is most opposed to Christian morals. He was a thorough-going hedonist, and therefore in poverty and suffering he could see neither beauty nor any possible value. Palpable well-being, such as the sight of a fruitful orchard may suggest, and as William Morris imagined (too æsthetically no doubt, for Butler's taste) as the reward of pleasant companionable labour—he would recognize no ideal less homely and 'objective' than this. The happiness of affection between kind, strong, amorous, beautiful people, among whom there is much kindness and little grief—that was his ideal; and it is one which, translated into terms of everyday life in a complex civilization admits of no contempt for wealth. Votaries of that earthly happiness inevitably see in the transcendental a dangerous lure, and in one who would 'lose himself in a mystery and pursue his Reason to an *O Altitudo!*' a natural enemy. They distrust and dislike ideals which minimize the comfort of what is assured. This emotion underlay all Butler's literary and artistic preferences and aversions; his depreciation, for example, of Plato, Michelangelo and Beethoven. He could never forgive the artist or poet who refused to kiss the earth; and his devotion to Shakespeare was, one suspects, due largely to the fact that Shakespeare is, after all, 'the surest refuge from the saints'. In Butler's mouth the theological word 'grace', compared with which knowledge and other qualities were unimportant, took on a pagan meaning:

> And grace is best, for where grace is, love is not distant. Grace! the old pagan ideal whose charm even unlovely Paul could not withstand, but, as the legend tells us, his soul fainted within him, his heart misgave him, and, standing alone on the seashore at dusk, he 'troubled deaf heaven with his bootless cries', his thin voice pleading for grace after the flesh.
>
> The waves came in one after another, the sea-gulls cried together after their kind, the wind rustled among the dried canes upon the sand banks, and there came a voice from heaven saying, 'Let My grace be sufficient for thee.' Whereupon, failing of the thing itself, he stole the word and strove to crush its meaning to the measure of his own limitations. But the true grace, with her groves and high places, and troupes of young men and maidens crowned with flowers, singing of love and youth and wine—the true grace he drove out into the wilderness—high up, it may be, into Piora, and into suchlike places. Happy they who harboured her in her ill-report. ('Note Books', pp. 38–9.)

Yet, at the close of the second chapter of *Life and Habit*, from which this passage is taken, he directs the reader who would have further understanding on all that is most important in life to believe in the music of Handel, the painting of Giovanni Bellini, and in the thirteenth chapter of St. Paul's First Epistle to the Corinthians—counsel which he repeated in various forms again and again. So, according to Butler, St. Paul after all must have had the root of the matter in him. It was Paul the Apostle of Protestantism of whom he was thinking in the foregoing passage. The Church, according to Butler, in her less introspective ages, in her buildings, her music, her un-spoken teaching, did uphold or at least sanction some kind of comely human ideal; and with the religion of the country people of Italy, who are described so delightfully in *Alps and Sanctuaries*, Butler felt at home. They at least made no attempt to be consistent and rational, and only a very moderate degree indeed of spirituality was demanded of them; above all, there was no 'earnestness' among them, no forcing of people to think that they were nothing if they were not at any rate 'colourable imitations of some one better than their neighbours'.

Never consciously to agonize; to undertake only 'that which insists upon being done and runs right up against you, hitting you in the eye until you do'—these were pre-cepts which he afterwards applied all round. In the case of Butler, his own philosophy made him a most amiable, trustworthy, amusing man.

Among imaginative writers, some have served us by turning our troubles and pleasures into tragedies and triumphs, showing life to us as a matter of momentous, immeasurable experiences, of which men are only inter-mittently worthy. With these, comedy is found in the inadequacy of man to his destiny; and at their hands disaster and death have often taken on a beauty more desirable than happiness itself. These are the magnifiers of life. Only when it is thus transfigured by the imagina-tion are its evils and its satisfactions tolerable: only then, they insist, do we see it truly. Their appeal is to those moments, whether of joy or grief, when common sense has looked foolish: such moments (and nearly everybody has, or thinks he has, experienced them) are the criteria by which they would have us measure the importance of things.

The other class of writers—and it is to this class that Samuel Butler belongs—may be described as the consolers. They diminish the importance of the issues at stake. They take the long-run, everyday estimate of things as the true one. They side with common sense. They find their comedy in the evanescence of aspirations, and in the spectacle of men protesting that they can only be nourished on ambrosial food while they are stuffing themselves with ordinary bread. If only men would not give themselves celestial airs, they say, they would be, perhaps, less amusing to contemplate, but they would have a far better chance of being happy and worthy of respect. Let a man find out really what he wants, and he will discover that it is something which exists on earth in satisfying quantities; something which the saints and the majority of the poets have unfortunately encouraged him to consider rather beneath his dignity. The former say, 'Throw not away the hero in your soul if you would get the most out of experience'; the latter, 'Cultivez votre jardin'.

Butler, as a philosopher and an imaginative writer, belongs to the tribe of Horace, Voltaire, Montaigne, Molière, and Fielding. To the idealist the tolerance of such writers towards humanity seems more insulting than the most violent misanthropy; and the quarrel between them, as Butler said of religion and science, is only to be reconciled in amiable people.

III

For the fame of Samuel Butler, Bernard Shaw did much, I did a little, and Festing Jones most of all. Fifield, the publisher, was also a great help in reprinting Butler's books, a work which has been continued by Messrs. Cape. Festing Jones helped to make Butler known long before he wrote his *Life of Samuel Butler*, which is the best piece of modern biography in the manner of the Dutch School, in which not only the sitter but his surroundings are painted in with careful and minute precision.

It may be said that from the day these two met in January, 1876, down to 1919, when the *Life* was published, their friendship circumscribed Festing Jones's life. Naturally, he had other interests, and other relations with people not directly concerned with Butler, but my impression when I first got to know Festing Jones was that even when he stepped outside the Butler sphere of influence, the spirit of 'Sam' was still upon him, deciding what he should feel, what he should value, and what friends he should choose. This was not so obviously true of him during the last ten years of his life, but for a good many years after Butler's death the passport to Jones's intimacy was certainly an interest in Butler. During the first few years that I knew him we talked of Butler incessantly. Fortunately it is a wide subject, with many ramifications and peppered with jokes; but I used to feel sorry for his sister, Miss Lily Jones—not that sympathy deterred me. Still, sometimes, as a great treat for her, I used to turn the conversation on to other topics.

His quiet and demure precision of utterance reminded me of Butler; also his deliberate politeness and his black, non-committal, respectable get-up. They both seemed to

B

declare, both in dress and behaviour, 'I am determined to be quite respectable'. Neither of them were anything of the kind. I do not wish to give the impression that Festing Jones was a pale copy of his friend, but he was saturated in him. He was always aware, and later he became more so, of a difficult and sometimes fierce crankiness in Butler which was foreign to his own nature, and although he half-admired this in his friend, he never imitated it. He did wish sometimes Sam had not been quite so crankily fierce. He began to respond, as time went on, to the work of musicians, poets, and writers whom Butler himself had no patience with, and to understand them without being overawed by his friend's limitations. While Sam lived, there was only one musician for both of them—Handel. Those who have read Festing Jones's two little books of travel, *Diversions in Sicily* (Alston Rivers) and *Castellinaria* (Fifield), will see that these quietly mischievous and affectionately observant books, though they owe much to *Alps and Sanctuaries*, are also the expression of an independent temperament, yet, most clearly, a temperament with which the author of *Alps and Sanctuaries* would have been in sympathy. Festing Jones had a very pretty wit, and among Butler's papers, out of which the 'Note Books' were constructed, are many acute and amusing remarks by him.

IV

He was a perfect friend. Butler might have said of himself, 'Two friends I have of comfort and despair'. It is Butler's account of the latter friendship, a most curious and painful story, which Mr. A. T. Bartholomew has given me permission to publish in this number. Butler also wrote an account of his friendship with Festing

Jones, which I hope to publish later. One anecdote will illustrate the closeness of their association.

A friend of mine, who was unacquainted with Butler and had never heard of Festing Jones, thought he recognized Butler from a photograph on board a Dover-Calais boat. He went up and spoke to him. 'Yes,' Butler replied, 'I *am* Mr. Butler, and Jones is down below.'

After Butler's death, Festing Jones organized a yearly Butler dinner, at which admirers of his works, and his old friends, met together, made speeches, and exchanged reminiscences. At first the attendance was small, consisting only of people genuinely interested in Butler. When the occasion became important, and the dinner crowded, Festing Jones, with characteristic discretion, stopped these celebrations. On the menu there was always printed, at the bottom of Butler's photograph, a sentence from his works:

> Above all things let no unwary reader do me the injustice of believing in *me*. In that I write at all I am among the damned. If he must believe in anything, let him believe in the music of Handel, the painting of Giovanni Bellini, and the XIIIth Chapter of St. Paul's Epistle to the Corinthians.

The quotation used to remind me of the story of the Chinese rationalist sage whose coffin levitated and remained suspended, until in answer to the urgent prayers of his disciples it sank slowly to the ground.

V

Butler's friends were much more important to him than women. Miss Savage was the only woman who meant much to him, and she only because she was witty and he fancied she was in love with him. He worried himself unnecessarily about this. Referring obviously to his over-scrupulousness in money matters, she had once written: 'I wish you did not know right from wrong', and this he afterwards interpreted as a reproach for his backwardness as a lover. In 1901 he wrote two sonnets about her, excusing himself: one cruel, the other touching, both having for a theme,

> A man will yield for pity if he can,
> But if the flesh rebels what can he do?

Butler was a man to whom continence was impossible. But he never fell in love with a woman; women represented a necessity for which he paid. This must be known if he is to be understood; and happily nowadays such things may be mentioned. The sex impulse was unusually strong in him from boyhood to old age, and he canalized it in that prosaic way which some men adopt who dread emotional disturbance in their lives. To the woman, who figures as 'Madam' in his biography, whom he used to visit twice a week, he did not even tell his name until he had known her for more than ten years; so great was his caution, so entirely had he disassociated intimacy from such relationships. When he was an old man he told me that now they had become impossible, unless he had 'a kindly feeling for the woman', but that it had not been so when he was younger. Nature took her revenge. The divorce between flesh and feeling lead in his case to one or two of his friendships being flushed with an emotion he hardly understood himself, and would have repudiated if he had. It is necessary to remember this in reading the strange story which follows; in addition, that in Butler's eyes Pauli was 'a swell'. Readers of *The Way of All Flesh* will remember the dumb and helpless admiration that 'Ernest' felt for Towneley, and his easy, confident, graceful ways and appearance.

There are only slight indications in Butler's account of the suffering this friendship brought him, but he has left a sonnet which I think, possibly, was born from it. He called it 'An Academic Exercise', and he wrote it to refute the theory of Sir Sidney Lee that Shakespeare's sonnets were only 'academic exercises'.

> We were two lovers standing sadly by
> While our two loves lay dead upon the ground;
> Each love had striven not to be the first to die,
> But each was gashed with many a cruel wound.
> Said I: 'Your love was false while mine was true.'
> Aflood with tears he cried: 'It was not so,
> T'was your false love my true love falsely slew—
> For 'twas your love that was the first to go.'
> Thus did we stand and said no more for shame
> Till I, seeing his cheek so wan and wet,
> Sobbed thus: 'So be it; my love shall bear the blame;
> Let us inter them honourably.' And yet
>   I swear by all truth human and divine
>   'Twas his that in its death throes murdered mine.

CHARLES PAINE PAULI AND SAMUEL BUTLER

Il est plus honteux de se défier de ses amis que d'en être trompé.
La Rochefoucauld, *Maximes*, 84.

Charles Paine Pauli, the course of whose intimacy with me will be detailed in the following pages, was born April 30, 1838 and hence was as near as may be 2½ years younger than myself. He was the youngest child of Emilius Pauli of Lübeck, who had settled in England and married a Miss Berjew, daughter to a Dr. Berjew of Bristol.

Dr. Berjew was of French Huguenot extraction, the name being an English corruption of Berjou. Mrs. Pauli was an only child, and her father's not inconsiderable property was settled on her, with remainder to her children. Emilius Pauli was in some kind of business in London, and at one time was, or was supposed to be, very well off, but either he failed or his business fell away about 1866, and during the later years of his life he was dependent solely on the income from his wife's marriage settlements.

His eldest son, whose name I forget, though I knew him in New Zealand as Resident Magistrate at Kaiapoi, had been in the navy and had distinguished himself more than once. On leaving New Zealand he entered the British consular service, and again highly distinguished himself, more especially at Barcelona during the disturbances that occurred there some 20 or 25 years ago. He and his wife both joined the Church of Rome, and he became closely intimate with the Duke of Norfolk, who watched over him night and day during his last illness, and seems to have been as devoted to him as I was to his brother Charles.

The second son, now Colonel Pauli, the only one of the family who survives, served many years in India. He was reckoned one of the handsomest men in the army and was liked wherever he went.

There was one daughter, who I have heard say was a great beauty, but refused offer after offer, and in the end joined a sisterhood. She was drowned when bathing at Mt. St. Michel, either in 1874 or 1875, while I was in Canada.

I think there were one or two other children who died young, but those I have named were the only ones who reached maturity.

As for Charles Pauli, I saw him once or twice at the club at Christchurch, New Zealand, in the early months of 1863, but he made no impression upon me, and I never spoke to him till thrown into contact with him at the office of the *Press* newspaper, then edited by James Edward FitzGerald. Pauli was a great favourite with Mr. and Mrs. FitzGerald and all their children, especially with their eldest girl Amy, whom I feel convinced that he would have married as soon as she was old enough had he remained in New Zealand. She was a very fascinating child, but as yet was only about 14 years old though she looked nearly full grown; it was hard, however, to say whether he was more devoted to the mother or to the daughter. Pauli was sub-editor of the *Press* at a salary of £150 a year.

I liked Pauli very well, but was not more drawn to him than to half a dozen others in one part or another of Canterbury, until one evening in September 1863 he called on me at the Carlton Hotel on the Papanui Road, and stayed till midnight. His visit was unexpected: I had not called on him and had no intention of doing so; I was surprised at his calling on me, but he was doing his best to please, and when he left I was aware that I had become suddenly intimate with a personality quite different to that of anyone whom I had ever known.

He had been at Winchester under Dr. Moberly. I have a high opinion of Winchester now, but I had a higher then. He had taken his degree at Oxford, and we Johnians looked on Oxford men as being a good deal above ourselves, at any rate in outward appearance and address. I knew myself utterly unable to get a suit of clothes that would fit me. Redfarn and Banham's clothes never fitted me when I was at Cambridge, much less did those made for me by Mr. Hobbs at Christchurch; while on my run I generally wore slop clothes ready made. Pauli's clothes must have cost at least twice as much as mine did. Everything that he had was good, and he was such a fine handsome fellow with such an attractive manner that to me he seemed everything I should like myself to be but knew very well that I was not. I knew myself to be plebeian in appearance, and believed myself to be more plebeian in tastes than I probably in reality was; at any rate, I knew that I was far from being all that I should wish myself, either in body or mind.

Everyone admired Pauli and thought highly of him. Wherever he went it was always the same. High and low were taken with the charm of his manners and appearance. I remember how the late Captain Buckley, V.C., told me that when he and Pauli were at San Francisco together in 1860 or 1861 they went into the bar of the hotel where they were staying, and the barman asked

Pauli to have a drink with him. Pauli tried to get out of it, but the barman said: 'Oh, but you must; you are the handsomest man God ever sent into San Francisco, so help me God you are!', with a strong emphasis on the 'are'.

In those days I knew very little of the world, and Pauli impressed me as especially strong precisely in those respects wherein I felt most deficient. I do not suppose that Pauli, after all, knew much more than I did, but so little did I know, that a confident manner and a good address were very readily taken for gospel by me. Perhaps the secret of it all lay in the fact of my knowing well that I had not passed by the ambush of young days scatheless, whereas I could see (and I imagine truly) that to Pauli there had been no ambush of young days at all. The main desire of my life was to conceal how severely I had been wounded, and to get beyond reach of those arrows that from time to time still reached me. When, therefore, Pauli seemed attracted towards me and held out the right hand of fellowship, I caught at it not only because I liked him, but because I believed that the mere fact of being his friend would buoy me up in passing through waters that to me were still deep and troubled, but which to him I felt sure were shallow and smooth as glass.

I was then nearly seven and twenty, and it goes without saying that I should have known more than I did, and been stronger than I was. Granted. But clerical surroundings and our much vaunted public schools and universities rarely impart that kind of *savoir faire* which stands a man in good stead when he goes out into the rough and tumble of the world. He is still a hothouse plant. Academic life will not seriously enfeeble those who are naturally robust, fond of games, and little given to thinking;

if on leaving the university they at once take one of the main roads towards which academic training generally tends, they will do well enough. But if they are not robust, if on leaving college they begin to think, and find, as I did, that the path which has been marked out for them is an impossible one—and my subsequent career has abundantly shown how impossible a clerical career would have been for me—if, after finding this, they drift into a position for which they have no kind of instinctive aptitude, then university training will have done them harm, at any rate for a time, till they have shaken it well away from them. In my own case it encouraged my natural conceit—a more utter young prig than I was at seven and twenty it would be hard to find—and did me harm in a hundred ways which there can be no object in detailing. Yet in the end, after many years, what I learned at school and Cambridge came back to me as bread cast upon the waters, and I am aware that I owe to Shrewsbury and St. John's no small measure of that success which I believe myself to have very sufficiently attained.

But let this pass. As I have said, when I first met Pauli I was younger than my years, and would catch at anyone whom I thought stronger than I was. How it happened that the £4400 I had had from my father had become £8000 in between 4 and 5 years, though it had reached me piecemeal, and some of it not till near the end of the time I was in New Zealand, I cannot conceive. The marvel is that I had not lost every penny of it, but so it was: my sheep had bred; wool had kept high and so had sheep; runs which were pretty cheap when I reached New Zealand had gone up greatly in value. I had got hold of mine bit by bit, and had pieced it into a compact, large, well bounded, and in all respects desirable property, but I was heavily involved with my merchants: I saw that if things fell, as they presently did, I might easily be cornered. I felt, moreover, that the life was utterly uncongenial to me, and I thought it wiser to sell, and go home, leaving my money out in New Zealand at 10% which was the rate of interest then current.

I was making arrangements with this end in view when Pauli first came to see me, and during the six or seven months which it took me to settle up everything, we were constantly together—I being devoted to him much as a dog to his master.

I soon found out that though he seemed so well and strong and handsome, he was really very ill. One day he showed me his tongue, and the skin was broken all over it. I supposed the mischief was syphilitic, but the doctors said it was nothing of the kind—it was only that he was thoroughly out of health. He kept getting worse and worse and suffering more and more, though he hardly ever complained, and bore great pain with that fortitude which he continued to show during many years of ill health to the day of his death. His pluck was indomitable, but I could see very well, and so did the FitzGeralds, that he was growing worse and worse. They, as fully as I, believed that he would die if he remained in New Zealand much longer, and I am as convinced now that he would have done so, as I and his friends generally were when it was settled that he should go home.

The plan was that he was to go home, recover his health if possible under English doctors, get called to the bar, and return to New Zealand (where I have no doubt it was intended that he should marry Amy), and practise there. The only drawback was that he had no money—

nothing, in fact, beyond a reversion to some £4000 or £5000 on the death of his father and mother, which was already in part anticipated.

I believed myself worth not less than £800 a year. What could be simpler than for me to say that I would lend him £100 to take him home, and say £200 a year for three years till he could get called and go out to New Zealand again? He was to repay me when he came into his reversion, and if more was wanted his father and mother might be relied upon to do it. To me, in those days, this seemed perfectly easy, and Pauli, I have not the smallest doubt, fully believed—for his temperament was always sanguine—that he would be able to repay me.

The plan was settled. We left New Zealand in June 1864 in an American barque bound for Callao. Thence we went up to Panama and to St. Thomas, where, or at Jamaica, I forget which, we joined the *Shannon*, whose captain, by the way, died before we reached Southampton. Pauli was very ill with his mouth and throat all the voyage, but no one save myself knew or suspected any suffering on his part. It was not till long after he reached England that he got rid of this, if, indeed, he ever did get rid of it, for after a time he would put me off, and would not show me his tongue at all. But over and above this he was always ailing.

We reached England in August 1864, and glad we were to do so. Pauli almost immediately found two sets of rooms, one at the top of No. 3 Clifford's Inn, the rent of which was then only £12 per annum, and another, the one in which I still live, in No. 15, of which the rent was only £23. It is still only £28, or about £36 in all including rates and taxes. Here we settled, breakfasting and generally spending the evening together.

All this time, however, I had felt—from the very beginning—that my intimacy with Pauli was only superficial, and I also perceived more and more that I bored him. I have not the least doubt that I did so, and am afraid he is not the only one of my friends who has had to put up with much from me on the same score. He cared little for literature, and nothing for philosophy, music, or the arts. I studied art, and he law. Law interested him, whereas it was nothing to me. He liked society, and I hated it; moreover, he was at times very irritable, and would find continual fault with me, often I have no doubt justly, but often, as it seemed to me, unreasonably. Devoted to him as I continued to be for many years, those years were very unhappy as well as very happy ones.

I set down a great deal to his ill health, no doubt truly; a great deal more, I was sure, was my own fault—and I am so still. I excused much on the score of his poverty and his dependence on myself, for his father and mother, when it came to the point, could do nothing for him. I was his host, and was bound to forbear on that ground if on no other. I always hoped that as time went on and he saw how absolutely devoted to him I was, what unbounded confidence I had in him, and how I forgave him over and over again for treatment that I should not have stood for a moment from anyone else—I always hoped that he would soften, and deal as frankly and unreservedly with me as I with him, but though for some fifteen years I hoped this, in the end I gave it up and settled down into a resolve from which I never departed, to do all I could for him, avoid friction of any kind, and make the best of things for him and for myself that circumstances would allow. For the last 15 years or so not an angry or unkind word ever passed between us.

But I am anticipating. I have no means of ascertaining how much Pauli had from me between the years 1864 and 1880 or 1881. I kept no accounts; I took no receipts from him; the understanding was that he would repay me when he came into his reversion, but there was no formal document, until about the year 1872 or 1873, he gave me, whether at my instance or his I cannot remember, an assignment of his interest in his reversion, to the extent of £2200.

I see from a letter I wrote to my father, Nov. 4, 1879, that I only admitted having helped Pauli from time to time; the fact was that I had done everything that was necessary to get him called, books, fees, etc., and to live. I had more than shared every penny I had with him, but I believed myself to be doing it out of income and to have a right to do it. After he was called, FitzGerald wrote to him pressing him to come out to New Zealand. He showed me this letter, and I said I thought he ought to go. To my unbounded surprise he burst into tears—a thing I had never seen him do, though I had done it often enough myself. That, from him, at that time was enough to settle the matter; but I was alarmed, for I had begun to be uneasy, as I well might, about money matters.

Pauli had long left Clifford's Inn. I do not think he lived there more than a twelvemonth. The place, he said, was intolerable to him, and he must have a more airy situation; so he went into lodgings in the West End. I am afraid I believe now that he left simply in order to get away from me. He came to lunch at my early dinner whenever we were in town together, i.e. nine months or more out of the year, but from a very early period after his settling in London the intimacy between us began to limit itself to this. During the first year or two we would sometimes go out of town together, but I always felt that he was bored and anxious to get away. In the autumn of 1866 we spent a month together at Dieppe, and at the end of it he said to me that though he believed I had been pretty happy he had never been so miserable in his life. After that I saw that going out with him did not, to use his own expression, 'figure', and we never, to the best of my recollection, went out with one another again, nor to any theatre nor to any place of amusement whatsoever.

When he changed his lodgings he left off telling me where they were, till I asked him; he did not like my coming to his lodgings nor to his chambers, and I gradually left off doing so. He kept his goings out and his comings in to himself as far as he could possibly do so. He once brought his friend Lascelles to lunch with me, as also Risley. Once or twice I met Swinburne, a friend also of my cousin Dick Worsley, at his rooms, I forget how or why; and after I had written *Erewhon* he took me to lunch with Mr. and Mrs. Swinburne. But year by year the more I did for him the more he kept me at arm's length, and for the last 15 years or so I did not even know where he lived—till I heard it on the day of his funeral. Of course I could have pressed him and insisted on knowing, or I could have found out in twenty ways if I had set about it; but I knew he did not wish it, and so utterly devoted was I to him, that I never questioned him, and when he was ill and I had to see his clerk, I never asked where he lived.

But this again is anticipating. I was beginning to get uneasy about money in 1869 or 1870, but it is so long ago that I cannot remember exactly. I did not like my New Zealand agent: I had had to take mortgages over, and the land which I had had to take, though it sold well in the end, was unproductive. All this is a story that haunts me and will haunt me to my dying day, for it was my great friend, W. S. Moorhouse, who was my mortgagee, one of the very finest and best men whom it was ever my lot to cross, a man who had shown me infinite kindness and whom I can never think of without remorse. Whether I could have avoided it or no, I do not, and did not, see how I could, without breaking faith with Pauli. If it was a trespass to call in the money, may I be forgiven as from the bottom of my heart I forgive Pauli for whose sake I did it. However, let it pass—it makes me sick to think of it. Bit by bit I called in my money, and invested it very largely in the companies recommended to me by Henry Hoare then head of Hoare's Bank and an old college friend with whom I had been intimate ever since my return from New Zealand.

I cannot remember when my money began to come, nor how long it was before I had entirely cleared out from New Zealand, but I have no doubt I infringed on capital during the years 1871 and 1872, though from the letter to my father of Nov. 4, 1879 I appear to have denied having done so. At that time, as I have said, I kept no accounts and hardly knew how I stood. I knew that my capital was still not materially impaired, but I also knew that I could not get the £600 or £700 a year which was wanted for the two of us from such investments as I could prudently make in England. I hoped, however, that Pauli would now soon get off my shoulders. I spoke to him to this effect but he said he only made enough yet to pay his chambers and clerk. I cannot remember what passed, or whether he even asserted this directly, but he gave me to understand it, and I unhesitatingly believed it, though I felt it keenly that I could get from him no even approximate statement of how much his earnings were.

The wrongness of Pauli's silence wounded me. I told him I thought it wrong, but he said he would tell me if he could—it was so difficult to say exactly what he was earning, people did not pay him, etc., and I, still believing him to be much as I was myself in the matter of good faith, accepted his excuses and made no doubt that if he had been able to ease me off he would have done so. I hoped, moreover, to sell pictures. I had had one or two in the Academy and was always hoping that I should get on as my fellow students were doing. I had also taken to writing, and *Erewhon*, if not already published, was close on being so. It came out in the spring of 1872, and the reception it met with made me believe that even though I had failed to make any money out of it, I should ere long be able to supplement my income very sufficiently by writing as well as by painting. Indeed, I did sell a few pictures from the Academy, and, being always sanguine, thought that I should be able to rub along very well, even though the income from my New Zealand money was considerably reduced.

If I had stuck to painting and never written any more, I believe I should have done very well. But alas! the success of *Erewhon* had fired me, and though for a time I felt as though I had said all I had it in me to say, it was not long before I remembered the pamphlet on the Resurrection which I had published in 1866, and set myself to develop it into *The Fair Haven* which was published in the spring of 1873. Dearly as I loved painting my mind now ran on literature to the full as much as on painting, and little by little I drifted away from painting, though for some years I still considered it as my main business.

If I had sold my picture 'Mr. Heatherley's Holiday' exhibited in the Academy of 1874, I believe I should have drifted back to the painting again, but my friends one and all told me that I was stronger as a writer than as a painter, and I suppose they were right; but they were wrong in thinking that the kind of writing in which I could alone interest myself would command a sale that would even pay its expenses.

There was also another disturbing influence. The companies in which Hoare advised me to put my money and which were to make us all rich men proved to be one and all of them worthless. The Canada Tanning Extract Co. was so promising that I gave Pauli back the assignment to me of his interest in his reversion, and he borrowed £1000 from Swinburne on it, all of which went into the C.T.E. Co. He also advised his brother, then Captain, now Colonel Pauli, to borrow £1000 (every halfpenny he could raise) and invest it in the same Company. Pauli and I were put upon the directory—this, I take it, was in 1873 —and at first everything was *couleur de rose*. By and by we found continual excuses from our agent in Canada and from the vendor, and it was decided in May 1874 that I should go out to Canada and report upon the situation. Furthermore, our faith in Hoare was demolished by his smash in February 1874, when it proved that he had speculated with and lost some £750,000.

As soon as I got to Canada I saw that the position was very grave. I will not go into the ins and outs of this long story, but must refer to a correspondence which I had printed between myself, the vendor, and the managers at the works,[1] which will show what a desperate fight I had,

[1] There are copies in the British Museum and at St. John's College, Cambridge.

and how completely I exposed the falsehood of those in whom we had placed our confidence. The Company could never have succeeded, for our extract of bark, though it made excellent leather, gave it a colour which was disliked in the market. The demand was practically nil, and week by week we were accumulating barrel on barrel of stuff which we found ourselves utterly unable to dispose of. I urged the directors to issue no more contracts for bark till we had found or created a market. It was of no use; and it was at this time that I first learned that Pauli had no backbone. I was in Canada, with the exception of, I think, two short visits to England, from August 1874 to November 1875. If my advice had been taken we should have saved a brand or two from the burning, but as it was, do what I might, I could not persuade the London board. In the autumn of 1875 they again issued contracts for some £30,000 of bark, and that was the *coup de grace*. I left the board soon after my return, and a few months later the Company went into liquidation. I do not believe even the debenture-holders ever got a penny back.

The correspondence between myself and Pauli during the time I was in Canada was very voluminous, but he either could not or would not look facts in the face. At his urgent request some six or seven years ago I returned him all his letters, and cannot now remember how and where he most especially failed me. I dare say he could not do much against Hoare and Whitley, who were obstinate as pigs, but the impression remains with me that he could have done much more than he did.

When I came back in the early winter of 1875 I was aware that I was ruined. I had still about £2000 left, and this Pauli and I set ourselves to eat up bit by bit.

I had learned a good deal about accounts in Canada, but I still did not keep them, and have no means of verifying what monies passed between me and Pauli till my capital was exhausted. I believe he had from me more than £300 a year in 1876, 1877, 1878, and 1879. All I know for certain is that I shared with him, and more than shared with him, to the last penny (or practically the last penny) that I could command.

I kept on writing, first *Life and Habit*, and then *Evolution Old and New*, and painting as well as I could, but though I wrote, so far as I can judge, better and better, I painted worse and worse. I was assiduous at dear old Mr. Heatherley's School—the very last thing to help me—but people said that my work was 'jaded', and I have little doubt that it was so. The Academy would hang me no more, and by degrees I resigned myself to the conviction that literature was my stronger card. If I had known as much as I do now I should have known that such books as *Life and Habit* and *Evolution Old and New* could never possibly pay their expenses, for Darwin was then at the highest point of his reputation. To write them was to run my head against a stone wall as surely as it has been for me to write *The Authoress of the Odyssey*. I can afford to write these books now, and when my head comes against the wall I am unscathed. I could not afford to write as I did in 1876–1881; but afford to do so or no, I was bursting with what I wrote, and as it has long since all come right, I am very thankful that I was vouchsafed the power to write them. If in my books from *Erewhon* to *Luck or Cunning?* there is a something behind the written words which the reader can feel but not grasp—and I fancy that this must be so—it is due, I believe, to the sense of wrong which was omnipresent with me, both in regard to Pauli, the Darwins and my father, and also to my ever-present anxiety as regards money.

I have gone into this so fully as my only excuse for eating up my capital when I must have known what a ruinous course I was pursuing. It is easy to see this now, but it was not so then, and when I look back upon it all, I believe I should do much what I then did if I had to do it over again. For there was still my reversion to the Whitehall estate. My father had only to join me in cutting off the entail of this, and without costing himself a penny he could enable me to borrow such sum upon it as would, I did not doubt, keep Pauli and me going till we could be self-supporting. I will say more, however, about this when I get further on with my story.

Pauli's ascendancy over me—I mean my faith in him as a superior being, as one who was in all respects stronger and better than I was—was at an end with my return to England at the end of 1875. By that time I had found out that I was the stronger man of the two. As I look back on some of the sayings and doings of his that I have put down in my earlier books of Notes, I see them with different eyes to those with which I wrote them, but I have left them as I found them; there they fell, there let them lie. But I do not think that my affection for Pauli was any less than it was in 1863. I had been with him so long, and when he chose to make himself agreeable he had a charm of manner which, were he still living, and did I not now know things which I had no conception of till after his death, would draw me to him much as I was drawn in the first instance. Besides, I had given him my word not to fail him; I believed him to be utterly ruined if I did not keep it, and I fully hoped, year after year, that he would ease me off.

At Xmas or thereabouts in 1875 I spoke to him with the utmost affection, and told him that he ought to let me know more fully how he was doing at the bar and what chance there was of his being able to release me to some extent. I said: 'You ought to tell me, good or bad, that I may know better how I stand; I have kept nothing from you; I am sharing everything with you, and you ought to use like frankness with myself, whereas, in point of fact, I do not even certainly know whether you make enough to pay the expenses of your clerk and chambers'. I told him that he was estranging me and implored him not to do so.

Again he burst into a passionate flood of tears, but do what I might I could get nothing out of him, except a general impression that he was just covering his expenses, and a promise that in the course of the ensuing year he would be more explicit. I believed his distress to be due to his conviction of the gravity of our difficulties and of his utter inability to do anything towards lightening them.

Then came the worst years that I have lived. Month after month passed and he said nothing, and when Xmas 1876 came I was so much nearer the end. When the year had passed I said much what I had said at Xmas 1875. There was the same passionate flood of tears, and the same quasi-promise of greater openness, but of information nothing.

Xmas 1877 came. I was oppressed at all times with a sense of the utter iniquity of the treatment I was receiving, but my book; my foreign trip in the autumn to the Canton Ticino; my friendship with H. F. Jones, which was now ripening into intimacy; my own sanguine temperament, and lastly the fact that the time during which Pauli and I were actually in one another's company was limited to his lunching with me from 1.20 to 2 or 2.10 three times a week, enabled me to bear it. I never said a word to him to ask him how he was doing. It would have been far better both for him and for me if I had said outright that I would not and could not stand such treatment, but I never said anything of the kind. He was my guest; I had been so long devoted to him; I fully believed him to be powerless, and that he would go down once for all if I took my hand from under him. I believed him to be very unkind, or rather cruel, but I also believed that he would speak if he could bring himself to do so, and that his silence tortured him hardly less than it did me. At Xmas 1877 I again spoke. There was the same passionate flood of tears and the same quasi-promise of greater openness, but of information nothing.

Whether I spoke again I cannot remember, but I know that I never spoke except after the expiration of a year from the time when I had spoken last. On one of these occasions he said he knew he ought to have said more by way of thanks than he ever had said, but that his pride forbade him to do so. On this I said the only bitter thing that I believe I ever said to him. I said: 'Pauli, that is not well said. Your pride never hinders you from receiving an obligation and if it were of the right sort it would not hinder you from acknowledging it.' He said nothing, but presently he said: 'I know I shall die without ever having said what I ought to have said, and if I do I shall suffer the agonies of the damned.'

I knew that he had a dumb devil, and pitied him; but I did not yet realise that a dumb devil is one of the most deadly that can take possession of any man. I did not want his thanks. I had not, and never had any other wish in connection with him than to help him to a position in which he might keep himself in comfort and perhaps distinguish himself. Able he certainly was; I never saw the slightest sign of snobbishness in him; I never heard him speak in a manner unworthy of a gentleman; whenever I appealed to him for advice on any subject I found him careful, attentive, and sensible. I refer to questions of law, and I have been told by those who knew his work that if it erred it did so in the direction of over-carefulness. I know very little of what he did, but I know that he settled the whole contract for the bringing of Cleopatra's Needle, and in spite of the many untoward accidents that befell the obelisk, Sir Erasmus Wilson found himself always on the safe side. This may not, perhaps, go for much, but I am satisfied, and always was so, that what work Pauli got he did carefully and well. The having no doubt on this head went a long way with me. What though he did not ever again go so near thanking me as he did on the occasion above referred to (and he never did), by this time I had given up all hope of his ever breaking through his reserve, except superficially, and it was becoming easy to me (and it gradually became more and more so) to do the best I could for him and leave him in all things to his own ways absolutely— believing firmly that he was doing all he could and that when better times came he would ease me off, if not repay me as much as he could.

So things went on between us till the autumn of 1879. Some time between 1874 and 1879 I came in for a windfall of £475 on the death of General Freer which staved off the evil day for a little longer, but in the end the day came. I seemed to have gone back in my painting and could not sell; my books made matters worse. The only card I had was my reversion to the Whitehall estate, of

which my father was now in possession. I could not
borrow money on the reversion until the entail was cut
off, and borrow money I must.

My father would not hear of cutting off the entail, and
insisted on knowing the details of my expenditure, of my
losses, and of my connection with Pauli. These I stated in
the letter already referred to, and dated Nov. 4, 1879—a
letter which I showed to Pauli before I sent it. The up-
shot of it all was that I undertook to do no more for Pauli,
and was to receive an allowance of £300 a year from my
father, less anything I could make for myself. At the same
time my father said he should only leave me a life interest
in any land he left me on his death—and he kept his
word.

I cannot say how much Pauli had by this time had
from me, but I am confident that it must have been
nearer £3500 than £3000, and I felt that I had long since
done all that I had ever undertaken to do, i.e. to see him
called to the bar and well started as a barrister. If I had
had more money now, or could have got the loan of it, I
should have shared it with him, but I was powerless, and
I was not responsible for his continued failure to make
anything at the bar. I had kept him a full ten years after
he had been called, and though I regretted it very bitterly
I could do no more. Besides, I had such confidence in his
adroitness and *savoir faire* that I felt tolerably sure someone else would help him if I did not.

Pauli behaved quite well. He accepted the situation
with the same absence of effusion that he had maintained
hitherto. As he had hardly ever said a word of thanks, and
as, to do him justice, he had never directly asked me for
money, or directly said that he must make shipwreck if he
did not get it, so he made no complaint nor showed any

desire to reproach me when it was forthcoming no longer; but I noticed that the coat in which he came to luncheon now was one the like of which he would have cast off long ago had not my supplies failed; and I noticed that his health, which, of late years, though never good, had been somewhat better, was again obviously declining. The most apparent sign of this was his cough, a cough which in the course of years robbed him entirely of one lung and so much of the other as at last to kill him.

Matters went on in this fashion for about a year and a half. My father repeatedly taunted me with 'living in idleness' upon him. I was working as hard as any man could work, and should, I doubt not, have made myself a good position and a sufficient income by my pen had it not been for my quarrel with Mr. Darwin, and the way in which I refused to let him ride roughshod over me. *Life and Habit* had been bad enough, *Evolution Old and New* was greatly worse, while *Unconscious Memory* was utterly intolerable. The opposition, not to say gross calumnies, of the entire scientific world created such a strong feeling against me that no one would believe I had anything to say that was worth reading, and my books were still-born, or nearly so, as they fell one after the other from the press. My father sided at once against me. I since found that he had himself quarrelled with Charles Darwin as a young man, and had in reality no greater love for him than I had; but he was one of the powers that be, and for me to set myself up against one of these was near akin to my doing so against himself. If I could write, why did I not write a novel or something that would pay? Why go and fly in the face of the most powerful literary clique in England when I ought to be thankful to be a hanger-on of the meanest of them? This was unanswerable, but

I could only do what I could do; and had I written a novel in the hope of making money, I am confident that, good or bad, it would have failed commercially just as my other books have done, and will do, for I always was an Ishmael and always shall be, and have no wish to change. Pauli all this time was cordially with me in private; he saw the iniquity of Charles Darwin's conduct, and never attempted to deflect me from the path I took.

I had the less compunction in sticking to that kind of literature which I thought would ensure me a permanent good name inasmuch as my father had no one to thank but himself if he had to make me an allowance. He had only by a stroke of the pen to cut off the entail of the Whitehall estate, and I was only too ready to get off his back then and there. I have no doubt some idea to this effect in the end occurred to him, for after about a year and a half, he asked me to take some Whitehall estate monies out of the Funds and to invest them in good securities which would yield a better income. Of course, I at once consented. The ink was hardly dry on the change of investment before he again flew at me, said that the allowance was too large and he should reduce it, and reproached me bitterly with my idleness.

I cannot be certain of dates within a month or two (for I am in Sicily away from documents and letters), but all the allowance I had from my father was £450, i.e. 18 months'; this is accurate. Then, one morning, to my great surprise, and without any solicitation from me, I received a letter saying that a further change was proposed in connection with the settlement of the Whitehall lands and monies; and when the proposed document came it was found to have cut off the entail. Pauli saw this at a glance, but I should not have known it if he had not told me.

Doubtless my father knew that others would find it out for me if I did not see it myself, and therefore said nothing.

I thought it safer to tell the solicitor that I saw the entail was being cut off by the proposed deed, and to ask him if this was intended. He replied that it was, and that he had proposed the cutting it off to my father as 'an act of justice' to me. I think it more likely that my father proposed it as a way out of having to make me any further allowance, but I was too glad to get the entail cut off to go beyond the fact that this was at last to be done, and said nothing. Then, shortly, my father wrote me a very bitter letter, and I at once went down to the 'George' at Shrewsbury and called on my father, saying that I would have no more allowance, 'and', I added very quietly, 'no more such letters from you as you have now sent me'. With that I left the house, but not seeing any reason why I should break with my father entirely I either wrote or called again, I forget which, to soften the effect of what I had said.

My scheme was to borrow £5000 or £6000 at 4½ per cent on my reversion, buy small house property that should pay me 7 per cent, mortgage my purchases, and buy more, continuing this operation as far as it was possible to do so. This, therefore, I proceeded to do. Unfortunately, I made all the mistakes that a man of letters who ventured on such a scheme would be likely to make, and as a natural result I doubt whether I ever made a penny over the interests I had to pay.

At the time of my investing, I believed Pauli to be in great need of money. I forget whether or no he told me that this was so; I think it probable that he never said anything directly, but he certainly conveyed the impression to me that he was in great difficulties. I was surprised that he had been able to hold out so long, and had been expecting a collapse from month to month. I knew I should get no information by cross-questioning, and that it would end in the same flood of tears on Pauli's part, and prolonged bitterness and sense of wrong on mine, if he said he would be frank about his affairs, and then let the year go by without a word, so I promised him £200 a year without any condition—on the understanding implied, though I should think never expressed, that unless he had this money he would be practically bankrupt and without profession. I did what I did simply out of pity, and to avoid that self-reproach which I knew I should feel if Pauli had to leave the bar while I had a shilling left. Had this happened, I know very well it would have haunted me as Moorhouse haunts me. I can forgive myself for having been the fool I was, and I can forgive Pauli for having let me indulge in such folly, but I could never have forgiven myself if he had been wrecked while I was able, at whatever cost, to help him.

My investing in house property led to my keeping accounts by double entry. Every penny, therefore, that Pauli had from me since 1880 or 1881 is duly recorded; the total exceeds £3000—I think it is about £3200, but say £3000. Pauli wished me to put it down in my ledger as though I received some consideration for the sums I paid him, and it was accordingly decided that they should appear in a superintendence account, as though Pauli managed the properties for me. But if any actual management on his part was attempted, which I greatly doubt, there was not even an attempt at it after three months—in fact it was not possible for him to practise at the bar and attend to a lot of house property at the same time; the account, however, remained 'superintendence', until it was closed on Pauli's death.

I had by this time fully recognized that anything worthy of the name of friendship between me and Pauli was not to be. I had no other wish in connection with him than to do the best I could for him, to avoid all further scenes, and to make him feel his dependence on me as little as possible. Our daily lunching together was cut down to three times a week, as more convenient to both of us. He would come at 1.20 and go about 2. We met at no other times. Any letter I had to write him was sent to his chambers. I talked freely about any subject that interested me; all conversation between us was perfectly friendly and genial; he saw that I meant it to be so, and followed suit; he was obviously trying to make himself agreeable, and often his advice was very sensible. I always consulted him on any matter about which I was in doubt, and to all outward appearance we were the best of friends; nevertheless I could see that it was an effort to him to be in my company at all, and knew perfectly well that the whole thing was a sham—on my part an endeavour to deny that my passionate devotion to him for so many years in times gone by was spent in force, and on his to satisfy himself that the intimacy between us was still so close as to warrant his taking money from me. Every quarter I gave him his cheque. He would smile apologetically and say, 'Oh, thank you', but no other allusion to money matters was made between us until it became necessary by my finding myself again on my beam ends.

I borrowed money here and there and staved off the evil day till about 1883 or 1884 when I was obliged to cut Pauli down to £100 a year, on the understanding that he could borrow the second £100 for a year or two from his brother, and that I would repay it on the death of my father. A second time we ate and ate and ate down to the bone, and in the autumn of 1886 I saw that by March 1887 my complete ruin was inevitable. On the 29th of November 1886, the day after his 80th birthday, my father was struck down with illness, and a month later he died.

It is an awful thing to say, but my main feeling on the death of my father was one of unutterable thankfulness. Never were two men thrown together in the relation of father and son less calculated to fulfil that relation satisfactorily. We were both of us good sort of people enough in our several ways, but we did not like each other. I never from my earliest childhood can remember any other feeling towards my father than fear and mistrust, and yet I always knew that in very many ways he was a better man than I was. As for him, he always felt that I was something that he could not understand, and whose ways of thinking were widely different from his own. But let that pass.

I had all along paid the interests on the sums I had borrowed on the day on which they fell due. It was now my unspeakable happiness to pay off the principal sums. My father left me very comfortably off, and I have never tried to make what he left me more, so that I have never been in money difficulties since he died. Curiously enough, on the day after my father's death, Pauli's father also died, aged 92, and he came into his reversion. He assured me, however, that when all his other debts were paid there would be nothing left for me. I said that if there was anything over he might keep it, and I heard no more of the matter.

All was now easy. I had, however, long feared that on

my coming into my property Pauli would expect me to do more for him, and once or twice I had said to him laughingly that I knew he would expect this, and knew also that I should not be able to do it. I had anticipated, one way and another, too seriously to forget the lesson I had learned, and was determined that being once set on my feet I would keep within my income. Besides, I was confident that Pauli had other friends as well as myself; and felt pretty sure that so long as he had £200 a year certain from me, he would, one way or another, make up what would be enough to keep him comfortably. I could let him have £200 without grudging it, and had found that he had rubbed on very fairly with this for so many years that I had no doubt he could continue to do so. I repaid Captain Pauli (with 5% interest) the arrears of the allowance that for the last few years he was supposed to have advanced; but it was to Pauli himself that I repaid them, and I greatly doubt whether it was not Pauli himself who had advanced them; this, however, I shall never know.

I kept to my resolution. Pauli never asked me for another penny; once or twice, indeed, he complained of being 'd—d hard up', but I turned a deaf ear, and laughingly said that I was very sorry that I could do nothing to help him. I was still fond of him in a way, and was determined that nothing but death should end relations between us. I always feared that I was unjust to him, and that if I knew all I should see that his difficulties were far more serious than I imagined, but I was resolved that I would do no more until I did know all. What I feared most was that he might have a wife and children of whom I knew nothing; and after having helped him to the end, I might find a family sprung upon me after he was gone, but I never asked him.

These last words assume a belief on my part that Pauli would not live very long, and in fact, by the time my father died, he was such a wreck in health that every winter seemed likely to be his last. His obviously wretched health and great suffering from his cough and breathing, borne with admirable pluck, was one of the greatest holds he had upon me. A more patient sufferer could not be. On his death I first learned that his lungs had been going for years. He never told me a word about this, and I supposed his cough to be like my father's, which was very bad indeed for many years, but did not prevent his living to be 80. Nevertheless, Pauli had death written on his face for years before he died, and though I made ample provision for him in my will, I had very little idea that it would ever take effect.

In the winter of 1889–1890, he had influenza so badly that, as I afterwards learned, his life was despaired of for some days. He communicated with me by letter through his clerk, never giving the address of the house in which he was living. Once or twice I called on his clerk at his chambers, 2 New Square, but did not ask where he lived. He begged me to leave him quite alone, and so managed that I did not know how grave his position had been till the main danger had passed. On his being able to be moved he went down to Bournemouth, returning towards the end of January; it was not till then that I was fully aware how ill he had been. Knowing that his expenses must have been very heavy, it was on the tip of my tongue to offer to help him, but I knew that if I once went beyond the £200 a year for which I was pledged, there would be no end to it, and determined to wait until he

C

asked me—which he never did. Moreover, as a matter of fact, I was at that time again living seriously beyond my income; this, however, did not last long.

After this illness it was plainer even than before that there was nothing to be done but to avoid distressing Pauli by allusions of any kind to money; to provide for him (which I had done) in the event of my dying before he did; and so to behave towards him at all times that I might never be haunted by the remembrance of any unkind word, should it turn out that I was the survivor. I am thankful to say that this consummation has been attained, and that my conscience is as void of all offence from me to him as it is clear from any feeling of bitterness towards his memory. He behaved very badly. I know it, but he was weak and ill, and I made wrong-doing fatally easy for him.

Every winter after 1890 he had more or less serious bronchitis, as he called it to me. Alfred, who used frequently to see him, thought him at death's door. So did I; but he always used to rally, and strangely enough in the autumn, and up to the middle of December, 1897, I thought him better and more likely to get through the winter fairly well than I had ever before seen him since 1890. He was, indeed, more *distrait* with me than ever, and I felt sure that he had something on his mind, but I left it to him to speak, and he never spoke. He would often let me say things to which it was obvious he paid no attention whatever; presently he would wake up, ask me to say it over again, and then give me his best opinion. This was very marked during the last two or three years of his life.

About three years ago, X, who had been a great friend of Pauli's, a man of very considerable means, but almost out of his mind for many years from excessive drinking, died. I had long fancied that X, who adored Pauli, might have been doing much for him what I had been doing (I had no idea as yet that he was intimate now with Swinburne), and was only too glad to think so. On his death, however, it proved that though he had appointed Pauli his sole executor, he had only left him a legacy of £200. On seeing his death in the *Times*, I said to Pauli that I hoped X had done something handsome by him. Pauli spoke as a man bitterly disappointed, but determined to take his disappointment like a gentleman. 'Of what use,' he said, 'is £200 to me? It will not even repay the £500 I owe Hoare's Bank—besides, I ought to give it to you'. If I had said I thought so too, I believe he would have given it to me; but I also believe he knew perfectly well that I should not take it. Of course I refused and laughed at him for offering it; it was the first windfall that I had known of his having, and I was glad that he should have offered it; but the idea of taking it from a man who had nothing behind him when I had £25,000 at the least —such an old friend too, and so bitterly disappointed into the bargain—was not likely to occur to me, and it certainly did not.

As an example of the opinion that this friend had of Pauli, I may say that Pauli told me he used to say that he, Pauli, had written *Erewhon* for me. When Pauli denied it he said, 'But you were a great deal with him and you talked to him'. Pauli said: 'I have been a great deal with you, and have talked with you often enough, but you never wrote *Erewhon*'.

I may add that for the last two or three years of Pauli's life both Alfred and I thought that he was better off: he would go out of town for a few days much more frequently, and just before Xmas 1897 he gave my laundress, Mrs. Cathie, 5 shillings, whereas he had never given so much as a sixpence before to either Mrs. Cathie or Mrs. Doncaster during all the years that he had lunched at my early dinner. I had always set this down to his great difficulties, for I believed and believe him to have been free enough with his money when he had any. I took no note of his supposed better circumstances, for I had years before made up my mind not to add to what I was giving him—nor to detract from it—till either he or I were beyond the reach of either receiving or giving.

And so matters went on, quite pleasantly, during the autumn and early winter of 1897. Pauli was very sympathetic about the reviews of my *Authoress of the Odyssey*—he evidently considered them iniquitous, and was, I think, more hurt and angry about them than I was, for he had expected a more cordial reception. He lunched with me on Wed. Dec. 15, apparently to the full in as good health as he had been for some time past, and he said he should come on Friday as usual, but on Thursday he wrote saying that I was not to expect him as he had caught a heavy cold and should not be at chambers till the following week.

This had so often happened before that I was not seriously uneasy. On Saturday Dec. 18, I received a line: 'I am going on all right, but shall not be about for a few days. Will write later on'. On Sund. Dec. 19, he wrote: 'I have bad bronchitis but am going on well now—still, I do not expect to be about this side of Xmas'.

I was now uneasy, but knew that there was nothing to be gained by my staying in London. If Pauli did not want me about him more than he could help when he was well, much less would he do so when ill. I wrote and said that

I believed the kindest thing would be to leave him quite alone, and that I proposed going to Boulogne for Xmas as I have done for many years past. If he wanted me he could telegraph and in four hours I could be in London.

I got an answer dated Dec. 22, in a nurse's handwriting, saying: 'Yes, you are quite right when you say that the kindest thing is to disturb me as little as possible. I am not allowed to write, but if you do not mind my using the pen of another, I shall be able to keep you duly posted from time to time. To-day I am really considerably better, and there is no reason now why I should not continue to progress. As to the other matter, please let it stand over'.

'The other matter' referred to the payment of £25, the balance of the £50 due to him at Xmas, for the half of his allowance had been anticipated early in December. I, thinking he might want the money, had asked him if I should send him a cheque.

I went to Boulogne on the 24th and on the evening of the same day another nurse wrote: 'Am going on fairly well, and should be much better if it had not been for these fogs. I am, of course, very weak'.

After this I had nothing more. On getting no news on the 27th, 28th, and 29th, I became sure that Pauli must be desperately ill, but I did not know that he was dead till I saw the announcement in the *Times* of Thursd. Dec. 30 that he had died on the 29th.

I was wondering when the funeral would be, and was about to inquire of his clerk at chambers when I received an intimation from the undertaker that it was to be on Sat. Jan. 1, and an invitation to attend. If I accepted we were to assemble in the Westminster Bridge Road close to the Necropolis station, and go down by special train to Brookwood Cemetery along with the body.

Among those present I recognised Lascelles, and Colonel Pauli, neither of whom I had seen for 30 years. I did not speak to Col. Pauli nor he to me, though I think he knew me. I had only seen him for five minutes on one occasion in 1866. As for Lascelles, I knew him because I could see traces of resemblance to a photograph of him which I had had in my rooms (in a group with Pauli and Arkell), otherwise I should not have known him. I knew no one else, and saw some men whose looks did not please me, especially one who announced himself repeatedly as Pauli's executor. This man struck me as one with whom Pauli should have had nothing whatever to do—others, whose names I did not know, looked like gentlemen, at any rate.

I introduced myself to Lascelles and he remembered me. We got into a carriage in which there was no one but a most respectable looking man whom I took to be one of the undertaker's men. I asked Lascelles where Pauli lived, for there could now be no reason why I should not do so. He answered that it was Belgrave Mansions, Grosvenor Gardens, S.W. (I forget the number). Presently the respectable man in the corner said to Lascelles: 'I think, Sir, you must be Mr. Lascelles; if so I have a letter for you from Mr. Swinburne—I am Mr. Swinburne's valet'. Lascelles took the letter and read it. I let the valet alone, knowing that Lascelles would be sure to question him as soon as he had read Swinburne's letter; and so it was, for Lascelles said: 'I wonder what made Mr. Pauli take to living there'. 'Mr. Swinburne', said the valet, 'persuaded him, for he lived there and wanted to have him near him. Besides the rooms were very cheap. He only paid £120 a year for them, which was less than he had been paying in Bruton Street.' This was a shock to me. I said to Lascelles, 'Have you any idea how much Pauli made by his profession?' He answered, 'I do not know how he has been doing of late years, but many years ago—perhaps 20, but I cannot be certain—he told me he was earning about £700 a year.'

I remembered how in 1879 my father wrote me that he had it from Edlmann that Pauli was making £1000 a year. I showed this letter to Pauli who indignantly denied it, and was again assured, or rather given to understand—for no definite statement did I ever get from Pauli—that he was making nothing over and above his expenses, beyond what it was absolutely necessary for him to spend if he was to get on at all. He had to make a certain show in order to get business. He should certainly get none if he did not. As for £1000 a year, it was of a piece with my father's saying that he (Pauli) was making £800 a year as editor of a paper in New Zealand. I did not press him farther, for I had the most unbounded confidence that he would not have done what he had been doing this 4 or 5 years past if he had not all the time been on his beam ends and in great danger of sinking.

It will appear presently that Pauli's greatest receipts in any one year were between £800 and £900, but that in the last few years his business had declined owing to his frequent illnesses, and that he had not taken more than between £500 and £600. My informant, Mr. Ainslie, the solicitor who is winding up Pauli's estate, gave me this information, referring to Pauli's account-book in my presence as he did so. I forgot to ask in which year it was that he made the maximum sum, but think it likely that it was a slight exaggeration of this maximum that became the £1,000 which Edlmann retailed to my father.

When I heard what Lascelles told me, my father's letter, to which I had never given a thought for so many years, came at once to my mind, and again I was very greatly shocked. Lascelles asked if there was any one to look after Pauli during his illness. 'Oh yes, Mr. Swinburne saw that he wanted for nothing; he had two nurses, and his doctor, who was an old schoolfellow of his own at Winchester. Everything that he fancied he had, but for the last day or two he could take nothing but grapes and champagne. The doctor thought he would recover till about 48 hours before he died, but he used to say, "They keep telling me I am better, but I feel a great deal worse." He used to like having me about him, and I would sit by his bedside and read the paper to him every afternoon. He was quite conscious till about six hours before he died, and he went off very easily in the end, at about one o'clock on the Wednesday morning.'

The valet was an excellent fellow, and no doubt treated Pauli much as my father's butler had treated my father, and as, I am sure, Alfred would treat me if I were ill; but the talk with him having become exhausted, Lascelles and I conversed further about Pauli. 'He was staying with me,' said Lascelles, 'a few weeks before his death to meet the Lord Chancellor, who was also staying with us, and when we were coming away at the station there was a porter who had helped Pauli with his luggage, but did not turn up to be tipped. Pauli was very much concerned and sent me a shilling for him by post, saying he should never be comfortable till he knew that the porter had got his bob. Now I thought that very nice of him. So many men would have gone away without ever giving the matter a thought.' I need hardly say that I said nothing *au contraire*.

Presently we reached Brookwood, and went to the mortuary chapel where the service was read with an unctuous affectation that I have seldom heard exceeded, and thence to the grave.

After the coffin had been duly lowered and the service ended we were asked to a luncheon which had been brought down with us from London. Everything was done regardless of expense, and I was wondering who in the world was paying for it—or, rather, I should have wondered if I had not heard from Swinburne's valet that Swinburne had been looking after Pauli; but I reflected with a certain grim satisfaction that for once in my life I was making a hearty meal at what was very nearly Pauli's expense. It was the nearest thing to a dinner from him that I ever had.

Presently the executor said to someone close by me, 'He has left his brother, Colonel Pauli, a thousand pounds', as though there were more than £1,000 to be disposed of under Pauli's will; and here the reserve, which I had maintained very sufficiently so far, broke down. I had been shocked at learning the style in which Pauli evidently lived and the amount he had been making at the bar while doing his utmost to convince me that he was not clearing anything at all. I understood now why Pauli had preserved such an iron silence when I had implored him to deal with me somewhat after the fashion in which I had dealt with him. The iniquity of the thing as it first struck me in full force upset me, and, calling Lascelles aside, I said I was in great doubt what to do. It seemed that Pauli was leaving money behind him; he had had between £6,000 and £7,000, first and last, from

me; ought I to tell the executor or no? Lascelles thought I
ought to put in a claim if I had any means of substantiating
it; but in a few minutes I had recovered my equilibrium,
and saw what I ought to have seen at once, i.e. that to
say anything would be both useless and undignified.
I said to Lascelles, however, 'Did he ever borrow money
from *you*?' 'No, never, not so much as a five pound note,'
was the rejoinder.

As for Pauli's leaving his brother £1,000, that was in-
telligible enough. It was to repair the loss Colonel Pauli
had sustained in the Canada Tanning Extract Co. I think
it more likely than not that Pauli had paid his brother
interest on this sum ever since the loss had been incurred.
I trust it may have been so. Moreover, I was glad to find
that Pauli had had £1,000 to leave; it relieved me from
all fear of his having been in serious difficulties during
the last few years of his life; and in a few minutes I had
decided to say no more to anyone about what Pauli had
had from me.

Presently we went back to the train, Lascelles and I got
into the same carriage, but after a time the executor,
Sam Bircham, a man named Preston, with whom it seems
Pauli used to go out yachting, but of whom I had never
heard, and Mr. Ainslie, who was by Pauli's desire acting
as solicitor for the estate, got into the carriage with us;
and the impression is rather strong upon me that they did
so with the intention of exploiting me.

The executor, who struck me as a very third-rate person
and who was in the farthest corner from me, asked me
if I knew anything about Colonel Pauli, and I said that
I had only seen him once but believed him to be a good,
simple-minded fellow. 'I say simple-minded,' said I, 'because I know that on one occasion Pauli was only just in

time to save him from personating a voter. His father had promised to vote for Marriott at an election for Brighton, and he being then very old, Colonel Pauli was starting to go and vote instead of him, without the least idea that he was doing anything wrong.' They all laughed. 'Well,' said the executor, 'he has taken £1,000 under his brother's will.' I answered promptly: 'I am very much relieved to hear it,' and the incident closed. Then we talked a little more about Pauli, his age, his health, etc., and I answered all questions genially; but I did not ask how much more Pauli had left, nor yet did I betray the smallest curiosity to know how in the world he came to have £1,000 to leave. At Waterloo Station we all shook hands and parted.

A few days later I resolved to write to Swinburne, being anxious to get some kind of acknowledgment that there was no further liability on my part in respect of the £1,000 which Pauli had borrowed from him and for which I had guaranteed interest. Pauli, a year or so after he had come into his reversion, had assured me that the £1,000 had been repaid, and I had taken his word for it; but I had nothing whatever to show to this effect, and was not quite easy as to whether I had not been made, in some way or other, liable for the principal sum. I therefore wrote to Swinburne, asking whether Pauli had left any kind of message for me during his illness. I said he had lunched with me for over 30 years, three days a week, up to the day on which he had been taken ill, and asked for any particulars of his last days that Swinburne might please to give me. Then I referred to my liability in respect of the £1,000, and said I should be glad of a line from him to say that this was at an end.

Swinburne wrote me at some length much what I had

heard from the valet. Pauli had mentioned no friends on his death-bed, and had been too ill to write, beyond executing a will which he had prepared beforehand, and which only wanted his signature. Swinburne told me of Mr. Bircham's attempt to see him, and of the extreme excitement it had caused him. He added that Pauli had been in a highly nervous and excited state during his illness; and I cannot help fearing that this was in some measure caused by fear lest I, too, should attempt to see him—for he never can have been quite easy in his mind about my not knowing where he lived, though he might very well have been so.

A few days afterwards Ainslie wrote me a letter returning me an old will of mine dated in 1864 or 1865, almost wholly in Pauli's favour, and which it seems Pauli had preserved, though he was fully cognisant of my later will —also now revoked in consequence of his death.

Some time later, perhaps in February, Ainslie wrote again saying he had found £1,000 of shares in the Canada Tanning Extract Co., and asking if I could tell him whether they were worth anything. He also said that he had several books and other mementoes of Pauli at his office, and if I would call he should be glad to let me take my choice.

I called in a day or two, being anxious to get as many particulars as I could. Also, I saw that Ainslie wanted to see me, for he must have perfectly well known that the C.T.E. Co. had gone into liquidation more than 20 years since. Moreover, I had already told Swinburne that I did not wish for any further mementoes of Pauli than those I had. On reflection, I had determined for the easing of my own mind to learn how much Pauli had left, and how he had come by it. I therefore determined to let Ainslie know what large sums Pauli had had from me.

After the ordinary preliminaries were over, he asked me as though casually, but I could see that he deemed the question important, whether I had known a man named X. I said that I had seen him once coming up some stairs as I was going down them, many years ago, but had never spoken to him. I added that I knew he had left Pauli £200. 'Yes,' said Ainslie, and the subject dropped.

Then I told him that though I had not the remotest intention of making any claim on the estate, and was speaking to him in the strictest confidence, Pauli had had sums from me amounting to between £6,000 and £7,000 in all, had been receiving an allowance from me of £200, paid quarterly, up to the day of his death, and that I had not even known where he lived till I learned this on the day of his funeral.

Ainslie was very much shocked. 'Now,' said I, 'Swinburne was also helping him?' 'Yes.' 'And he was keeping me dark from Swinburne, as he was keeping Swinburne dark from me?'

'It seems so.'

'And that is why he would not tell me where he lived?'

'Doubtless. Swinburne always wondered why he would never allow his name to appear in any directory except as of 2 New Square, Lincoln's Inn, and why he particularly desired that no other address should be given in the announcement of his death.'

I smiled. 'Silly, silly Pauli! just as if I could not have found out years ago if I had chosen to do so.'

I have since looked in the London Post Office Directory in the reading room of the British Museum and find Pauli's only address as 2 New Square, Lincoln's Inn. It is sure to be the same in all the directories, but I have not looked.

Ainslie *loq.* 'When you wrote to Swinburne that Pauli had been lunching with you three times a week up to the day he was taken ill, Swinburne was very much surprised, and said, "Butler? Butler? Why I have not heard of Butler for this twenty years past." I laughed and answered, 'Nor I of Swinburne.'

I then said I should be very glad to know, if Ainslie was at liberty to tell me, what estate Pauli had left, and how he had disposed of it by his will. I asked this out of mere curiosity, for I knew that I should have been told long since if he had left anything to me. Ainslie said he thought I had a right to know. The gross estate was £9,000 (or sworn under £9,000, I forget which). Roughly, legacy and estate duties, £500 owing to Hoare's Bank, and tradesmen's debts (which were considerable) amounted to about £2,300. £1,000 was to go to Colonel Pauli, £300 to an old servant of his mother's, £50 to his clerk, and the balance to a lady, a distant cousin, whose name I do not remember. I give the figures correctly, I believe, but they can be easily verified at Somerset House.

'And how,' said I, 'did he become possessed of this sum?' 'Heaven only knows,' answered Ainslie, 'I thought you might perhaps be able to tell me.'

'Not I. Was it well invested?'

'Excellently—it was chiefly in Armstrong's (and some other equal good security which I cannot remember). I ought to have asked whether Ainslie knew how long Pauli had had this money; in the shock of my surprise I forgot to do so, but if he had only had it recently I think I should have been told.

'Is it possible,' said I, 'that he speculated?' Ainslie answered gravely, 'I think it highly probable.'

It was now time to bring the interview to a close, and I said, 'You can tell Swinburne just as much or as little of what I have said to you as you think fit.' Ainslie said, 'It will be better to say nothing. Pauli is on a high pedestal in the opinions of Swinburne and all his set. It would shock them terribly if they were to know what you have told me. You say you have no legal claim on the estate, or, if you have, you mean to waive it. Pauli is dead, and after all there is a good deal in the old saying *De mortuis*, etc.'

I said that he was very likely right, and that I should say nothing more about it.

After I had left him I remembered that there were several people who knew that Pauli was to the end of his life in receipt of a considerable yearly sum from me, and wrote urging Ainslie to do his utmost to keep the value of Pauli's estate from getting into the papers. I have not seen it published, so I hope he may have been successful. I may mention that Ainslie hardly knew Pauli at all, and was very much surprised and rather flattered at being appointed, under Pauli's will, solicitor for the estate.

And now let me give my own idea as to the way in which Pauli came to die worth some £9,000. I do not believe he speculated, and I greatly doubt whether Ainslie believed it either. He said what he did to throw me off the scent. If Pauli had speculated he would never have left £9,000—he would have lost every penny of it, for he was a complete outsider. I think also that he realised what utter gambling speculation is, and was too shrewd to gamble. I may be wrong, but I do not think I am. If, however, he really did speculate, I feel sure that £9,000 is but the wreck of a much larger sum.

On thinking the matter over I remembered that Ainslie's first question to me had been whether I knew X, and it struck me with some force that he suspected Pauli's money to have, in some way or other, come from X's estate.

Years ago I remember Pauli's laughing to me about X, and the shifts he was continually trying to evade income tax. Also on X's death, or during the winding up of his estate, Pauli told me that large sums amounting to between £40,000 and £50,000 had disappeared without leaving a trace behind them. Pauli said he felt sure that X had been being blackmailed for years. The porter at the club had once spoken to him very seriously, as being known to be an intimate friend of X's, and had told him that men of suspicious character had come there asking for X and had hung about waiting for him on being told to go away. Pauli told me the porter had begged him to speak to X and warn him. This, I gathered, had been many years ago. For several years before his death he was paralysed and under the care of two men to each of whom he left £4,000, as well as a very considerable amount of jewellery which he had a strange fancy for acquiring. One of these men, according to Pauli, was a blackguard; the other a decent fellow enough had he not caught X's passion for drink. Both the men were supposed to be there partly to take care of X in his helpless state, and partly to keep drink away from him. Pauli did not think either of them had got hold of any of X's money by fraud or force, but he had been lavish to them at times, though naturally very stingy. Anyhow, the net result was that whereas X should have been worth some £120,000 or £130,000, there was not much more than half this sum to be found.

I do not know why Pauli told me all this, for he was generally reticent about other people's affairs as well as his own; but he told it me, and I suspect strongly that Ainslie was inclined to think that Pauli's money had somehow or other come to him from X's estate. He thought it possible that I might be able to throw some light upon the subject, and that, I take it, was why he sent for me. I am sure that till I told him the facts he had no idea that Pauli had been having money from me; but I fear on learning how the case stood, he may think it likely that Pauli was a good deal more able to explain what had become of X's money than he really was.

I believe every word of what Pauli told me about X. If money disappeared I have very little doubt it was got hold of by blackmailers. Pauli would never invent such stories. Unscrupulous as he was, he would draw the line at a categoric lie. If anyone would give him money, he would take it, without the smallest consideration for anyone but himself. He would play upon people to make them give it him, and I have little doubt he played upon X as he did upon me and Swinburne; but no power of mine was ever able to extract from him a categoric statement to the effect that he would be bankrupt if he did not get it. Money was to him like cream to a cat, but it must be given him, under fraudulent misrepresentation if you will, but still *given*, before he would take it; and I made it fatally easy for him to take it, as doubtless did Swinburne. When I made it plain that I was not going to let him have more than £200 a year, there was an end of the matter. He never put any pressure upon me beyond once or twice soon after I came into my money saying that he was 'd—d hard up'. I feel as certain as I am that I am now in Rome, that Pauli never had anything from X beyond what X chose to give him. I also feel pretty sure that X was not likely to give him very much during his own lifetime.

What I imagine happened was this. X expressed a desire to do something for Pauli—say £10,000 in his will. Pauli said, 'If you do this it will appear, and it will all go in paying legacy duty and a friend, to whom I owe several thousands, and who will expect repayment if he hears that I have come into so much money. Your bequest, therefore, will be of no benefit to me. If you wish to be of real service to me give me this money by deed of gift; I will invest it in such securities as you approve, and I will give you a document acknowledging that I hold them in trust for you during your life. Make me your sole executor so that I can destroy all traces of the transaction, leave me say £200 to save appearances, and leave the bulk of your money to your sister. You may be sure I shall pay you interest as long as you live, for you will hold my acknowledgement. You will thus cheat the government of legacy duty and benefit me effectually at one and the same time.' That Pauli only left £9,000 behind him instead of £10,000 was, I imagine, due to his having eaten up £1,000 or so, in addition to his income from all sources, during the last two or three years of his life.

The only other explanation that I can think of to explain the disappearance of the much larger sum than £10,000 from X's estate is that X speculated with it under Pauli's guidance and lost it—but this I do not believe.

I can now bring this squalid, miserable story to an end. On thinking it all over, my main feeling is one of thankfulness that I never suspected the facts as I now know them till after Pauli's death. The only decent end for such a white heat of devotion as mine was to him for so many years was the death of one or other of the parties concerned. If I had withdrawn from him and said I should do no more for him, I firmly believed that he would say nothing, leave me, and probably either blow his brains out or drown himself. I felt pretty sure I was doing a great deal too much, but I had rather have done a great deal too much than a little too little. Moreover, I knew him to be in wretched health, quite unfit to bear any great shock or change of habits. It was absolutely impossible for me to suspect that he had £9,000 solid money behind him. Knowing what I do now, I see that the withdrawal of my £200 a year would not have been the disaster to him which I thought it would; but even so, Pauli would never have stood my breaking with him. Not that he liked me—it is plain he never did so—but he respected me, and feared me. He must have feared things coming round to me. He would never have known what I might not say about him. Physically he was as brave as morally he was the reverse; if he had found himself threatened with disgrace he would never have faced it. This is my belief, and the more I think of it the more thankful I am that I never knew the truth until it was too late for my knowledge to tempt me into departing from the line of conduct which I had long decided upon.

Besides, even though Pauli had not gone under in consequence of my breaking with him, if he had died as he easily might in any of his winter colds years before the end actually came, I should have been haunted by the fear that I had been the cause of it to my dying day. Whereas now my conscience is absolutely clear of all offence towards him, save that of having made it so

deplorably easy to do things which, i
harder, he would have been less likely
is over: I am thankful that it is so. I
way in which Pauli hoodwinked me; :
Ainslie, though he left me nothing in h
effect, left me from £200–£210 a year
goings, for the luncheons must be taken
We both of us laughed somewhat heaɪ
in the luncheons.

How far I am right in leaving this re
action I am more uncertain. Jones thiɪ
it. I can at all events destroy it later,
taken advantage of my foreign trip tɪ
times now while the later incidents are :
I should never have written it at all. I
myself from the other work I have in ha
and able to get to the Museum. If ever iɪ
it should be remembered that it is an ɪ
and that Pauli's version of the matter ca
For I hardly think that he can have :
cerning any part of it.

Lastly I cannot refrain from remɪ
thorn Jeudwine was in my grandfather'
Mutatis mutandis it is a very singular
nearly the same length of time I sho
closely linked with one whose connec
on the whole, I suppose I must admɪ
have borne my cross with anything lik
command, surely that should be enou
Frid. May 20, 1898. (Begun about Aɪ
this rough copy.)

Note.—This narrative is bound up

Butler's MS. Note-Books. Some use was made of it by Henry Festing Jones in his *Memoir* of Samuel Butler, but it is now for the first time printed in full. Festing Jones attached to the narrative a letter which appeared in *The Times Literary Supplement*, 30th October 1919, from Mr. Sam Bircham, who had read the story of Pauli and Butler as given in the *Memoir*, which had then recently been published. Mr. Bircham's letter concludes: 'To read this record of Pauli many years after his death is to me very painful, and I wish to record my belief and trust in my dear old friend. There must be some explanation.'

There is also this note in Festing Jones's writing, dated 8th January 1928: 'If anything further is ever done about the relations between Butler and Pauli this Maxim of La Rochefoucauld must be used as a motto.' He then quotes the 84th Maxim. I have fulfilled his wishes.

A. T. B., August 1931.

UNPUBLISHED EXTRACTS FROM THE NOTE-BOOKS OF SAMUEL BUTLER

(With the permission of Mr. A. T. BARTHOLOMEW)

These notes are a very small selection from those written by Butler between 1874 and 1883, and revised and written out fair between 1891 and 1897.

IN ART. I, 3

Whatever has been once transcendent remains so, however much it be transcended later. All that is not transcendent dies and disappears—*exceptis excipiendis.*

CANADIAN JOKES. I, 4

When I was there I found their jokes like their roads—very long and not very good, leading to a little tin point of a spire which has been remorselessly obvious for miles without seeming to get any nearer.

EREWHONIAN DOCTRINE—RIGHT AND WRONG. I, 10

This is recognised when we say of a sick person that there is something wrong with him. All is wrong that is not normal. Either very wrong or so right as to be wrong.

SHAKESPERIAN FRAGMENTS. I, 11

'I say 'tis here, bring thy putty hither.'

'Nay, but if it be not *here*, I will eat both thee and thy putty.'

Copied about 1858 or 1859 from a Newspaper account

of a gas-explosion at Sheffield, and the inquest that ensued. I forget whether there was more or not, but I noted and copied the fragment just given.

FAITH. I, 13

What is faith but a kind of betting or speculation after all? It should be: 'I bet that my Redeemer liveth'. *Cf.* p. 1.

PAIN AND PLEASURE. I, 14

Pain and pleasure are infectious. It depresses us to be much with those who have suffered long and are still suffering; it refreshes us to be with those who have suffered little and are enjoying themselves. But it is good for us to be depressed now and then.

JUSTICE. I, 14

Justice is my being allowed to do whatever I like. Injustice is whatever prevents my doing so.

THE SEXUAL QUESTION

As regards the greater freedom which those who think as I do would allow the young of both sexes, with such precautions as the faculty may approve, we are met with pictures of the universal debauchery that would follow. This might perhaps have been true once, but the world is grown older and can be better trusted.

WORDS GET LICHEN GROWN AND

crumble like stones in an old wall, but it does not do to build a new wall with old stones to make it look like an old one. Let the new work age if it will and gather picturesqueness in its own good time.

GOD IS LOVE

I like 'Love is God' better.

CANADIAN RESTAURANTS

When the Canadians have a decent restaurant, they will be nicer people, and when they are nicer people they will have a decent restaurant.

I'M A PUBLICAN

An old country clergyman declaiming against modern scepticism declared that morality was all very well, but that it was not enough to keep men fairly straight. 'Morality,' he exclaimed, 'may do for some people—it may do for Pharisees—but I'm not a Pharisee. I am a Publican—Thank God!'

BEET ROOT AND MODESTY

The beet root is a better emblem of modesty than the rose. The colour is as fine; it conceals itself from the view more completely; moreover it is good to eat, and will make excellent sugar.

THE NATURE OF THINGS IN THEMSELVES

A thing '*is*' whatever it gives us least trouble to think it is. There is no other '*is*' than this.

A MAN IS SHORN OF HIS STRENGTH

if he belongs to one set or to one woman.

LIFE AND VIVISECTION

The life of some people seems rather a vivisection than a life.

THE GREATEST HAPPINESS OF THE GREATEST NUMBER

will be best promoted by increasing the prosperity of those who are now best and comeliest.

ART NOTE

A painter should find out what is the most important hundredth part of what he sees. If he can settle this justly he has painted his picture, to all intents and purposes.

THE ONE SERIOUS CONVICTION

that a man should have is that nothing is to be taken too seriously.

ART NOTE

When in doubt do as nearly nothing as you can.

WE ARE HIS PEOPLE AND THE SHEEP OF HIS PASTURE

We profess to accept with thankfulness the position of being God's sheep, yet few lambs are allowed to become full grown and it is not intended that any should die a natural death. A sheep's *raison d'être* is to be fleeced as often as possible, and then to have its throat cut.

Uriah the Hittite, if his own life had been spared, would no doubt have sat down to the little ewe lamb which he carried so tenderly in his bosom, and dined off it with much satisfaction; and when, again, we see pictures of our Saviour with sheep behind Him, and a lamb in His bosom, we should remember that the matter will not end here. If a shepherd caressing a lamb is a fair statement of the case, a cat playing with a mouse should be hardly less so. We may be asked to bless the grass, the sunshine and our fellow sheep, but can we reasonably be expected to bless the butcher? Is it not time to drop that metaphor?

KNOWING A LITTLE MORE OR A LITTLE LESS THAN WE DO

We like those who know much about the same as we do, or much more, or much less; but we do not like them to know a little more or a little less. Jones says the same holds good with money.

BIRDS' EGGS

Why do birds colour their eggs so beautifully for so short a time, and when it is not intended that they shall be seen by any but the parents? The sentimental turtle and the prosaic hen are alike satisfied to sit on a plain egg without going to the trouble and expense of colouring it.—Why can a hedge sparrow find no peace in anything short of turquoise? We are tempted to exclaim: To what purpose is this waste?

WOMAN AND HER POSITION

The case of a woman now stands thus. Every one of her ancestors for millions and millions of generations has been endowed with sexual instinct, and has effectually gratified it. For a longer time than our imagination can realise there has been no link broken, and hence no exception. The instinct has been approved, confirmed and made stronger in each successive generation. Surely she in whom it has been thus sanctioned may claim the right to gratify it should occasion serve.

'No,' says Society to the unmarried woman very sternly. 'Break the link, in your own person; stem the current of that passion to which both we and you owe our very being; run counter to the course of things that has led up to you, be indifferent to that which has ranked next to life itself in the heart of every mother from whom you are descended. If you even attempt this more than Herculean task seriously, we will not honour you, but will laugh at you for an old maid; if on the other hand you are disobedient, we will chase you out into the streets and call you infamous.'

And then we are surprised that women are not at all times exactly what we could wish.

ART NOTE

To impress a form on one's mind when one has nothing to draw with, trace an outline on the palm of the left hand, with the right forefinger.

WHAT IS BEING IN A PLACE?

Am I more in the Sistine Chapel when I have first rate photographs before me of the frescoes it contains, and can study them at my leisure (not that I have the smallest wish to do so), or when I am in the Sistine Chapel itself on a dull winter's day and pressed for time? The Sistine chapel is more in the autotype gallery in Rathbone Place than it is at Rome.

So again he that is examining the moon through some great telescope is more in the moon than he is on earth.

THE IMPORTANCE OF LITTLE THINGS

This is all very true, but so also is the unimportance even of great things—sooner or later.

GOD

A writer in the *Pall Mall Gazette*—I think in 1874 or 1875, and in the autumn months but I cannot now remember —summed up Homer's conception of a God as that of a 'superlatively strong, amorous, beautiful, brave, and cunning man'.

This is pretty much what a good working God ought to be, but he should also be kind and have a strong sense of humour. After having said the above the writer goes on: 'An impartial critic can judge for himself how far, if at all, this is elevated above the level of mere fetish worship.' Perhaps it is that I am not an impartial critic, but if I am allowed to be so, I should say that the elevation above mere fetish worship was very considerable.

SILENCE

There is none so impressive as that of a hushed multitude.

REGENERATION

The only true is re-creation: I do not want to be re-generated otherwise than by being refreshed and amused.

MUFFATEES — HOW DO YOU LIKE YOUR?

One night some years ago I was at the Globe Theatre, and the Prince of Wales (Edward VII) came in. He was unpopular about that time in consequence of the Mordaunt Divorce case which was then on; it had come out in evidence among other things that Lady Mordaunt had made the prince a pair of Muffatees. There was a little hissing when he came in, which subsided, and then a voice from the pit, near me, sang out: 'How do you like your muffatees?' The prince smiled, and the feeling of the house at once went round in his favour.

DETECTIVE POLICE OFFICER WITH PRINCE OF WALES AND FRIENDS

The Prince was fond of going the rounds with the police, and did so once with a few others, among whom there was a mere lad who nevertheless saw all that was to be seen. Before separating they liquored up, and the boy said to the detective who had gone round with them: 'Now you think yourself a very sharp fellow, I know.'

'I don't know about that, but when I've seen a person once I generally know them again.'

'I'll bet you, you don't know who I am.'

'I beg your Ladyship's pardon,' was the rejoinder.

REASON

Our reason teaches us that the foundation of things is something abhorrent to our reason: for it points to a self-renewing motive power—that is to say, to perpetual motion.

CARLYLE AND PLATO

I don't like Plato, but I suppose I prefer him to Carlyle.

CULTURE

A man should be just cultured enough to be able to look with suspicion upon culture, at first, not second hand.

BOOKS, MY

When anything in them is rather strange and *outré*, it is probably drawn straight from nature as close as I could draw it; when it is very plausible, there is probably no particular and especial foundation for it.

AUNT BESSY

My mother's sister, Aunt Bessy, is what they call a person of weak intellect—her intellect may be weak, but if she wants one thing and every one else another, it is the every one else who has to yield, not she. Once she was at Taviton Street and my Aunt Philip had fairly fled, leaving Alice as mistress of the house. It was Summer, and after dinner the dessert was not to Aunt Bessy's liking. The nervous twitching motion in her head showed that she was much displeased, and at last she spoke. If your mother had been here' (twitch), 'Alice' (twitch), 'there would have been strawberries: there would have been strawberries' (twitch), 'Alice' (twitch), 'if your mother had been here' (twitch). 'I am your Aunt' (twitch), 'and it is not right; it is not respectful, Alice' (twitch), 'that there should not be strawberries. It is the time for strawberries, Alice' (twitch), 'and if your mother had been here', etc. No one could say a word, and she hammered away with a persistence that the strongest intellect might envy.

She lived 40 years with a Miss Evans, at Tavistock, and the two got on very well, but a few months ago Miss Evans was taken ill and was evidently going to die. Aunt Bessy has a great fear of death, so she insisted that the connection should end at once, and she came up to my Uncle's at Chester Terrace, pending other arrangements. She insisted that she should not be told if Miss Evans died. She said to Amy 'it is much better for me, Amy, that I should not know if Miss Evans is dead', and no one dared tell her when she did die—which she did soon after Aunt Bessy had gone.

In the course of her life she had accumulated household

gods to the extent of one box and a whatnot. In this she keeps her doll and her toys. She is about 73 now, but believes herself to be pretty: 'I hope they will say, Amy, that the pretty lady' (twitch) 'the lady with the pretty brown hair, Amy' (twitch), 'has been here.' When she went to Clifton she sewed up £8 in her petticoat. (She died, I think, last year (1895), aged about eighty-five. She said it was very uncomfortable to make a Will, so she died intestate, whereby I took some £700 which I should never have received otherwise.)

DICKENS' HOUSE

On one of our Sunday walks Jones and my Cousin and I were at Gad's Hill: an American tourist came up and asked if that was Charles Dickens' house—pointing to it. I looked grave and said: 'Yes—I am afraid it was', and left him.

MYSELF AND POSTERITY

Posterity will not have imagination enough to tell it what a fool I am, and if I dangle enough works before it, it may be caught by some of them. Why I should wish to trouble posterity—what harm it has done me for which I would punish it—what good for which I would reward it—I know not; all I know is that I mean catching posterity if I can.

MISS SAVAGE AND THE SELF-HELP CLUB

She said they were called the Self-Help Club, because they helped themselves, and they were the only people whom they did help.

PHYSICS AND METAPHYSICS

There is no drawing the line between physics and metaphysics. If you examine every day facts at all closely you are a physicist; but if you press your physics at all home you become a metaphysician; if you press your metaphysics at all home you are in a fog.

For example, we say such and such a thing is so and so. But what is 'a thing'? Strictly speaking, there is only one thing—the universe—all other things are called so through arbitrary classifications like species, and tend to vanish as 'things' if examined with any closeness.

The difficulty is to know where to stop in what direction. There is so much to be got by study within due limits, and so much to be lost by going beyond them; and so often an enquiry which at first seems very profitless has developed great results. Where is the line to be drawn? That is just what every one must settle for himself, and be a fool or otherwise according as he has settled it well or ill. There can be no rule given for drawing lines. As material things prove all to be connected and parts of one thing—as the pebble at our feet and the most remote and profitless fixed star are still united, so 'does it rain, my dear?' and the most dreary metaphysical enquiry are still closely connected.

LIFE AND HABIT

One aim of this book was to place the distrust of science on a scientific basis.

CPSIA information can be obtained
at www.ICGtesting.com
Printed in the USA
BVHW01s1441060218
507391BV00010B/86/P